Some Things Need Said

A COLLECTION FROM A LIFETIME OF POETRY

KELLY OLIVER

AMAPUBLISHING

Contents

Listen To Me

My Teddy listens to me
But he doesn't feel
But he listens
And he doesn't think bad of me
If only Maggie was here
She listens
And she feels
But she's gone
I need someone to talk to
Who will listen
And feel
But not think bad of me
Only animals listen
The ones I love
Maggie
My horse
Teddy, but he isn't alive
People listen
And they feel
But they think bad of me

And God
He listens
And feels
And forgives
I just need someone to listen to me
How can I talk to people
When they look
And stare
And have their own opinion
Maggie listened
And cared
But she's gone
Only Teddy is there
To listen to me

March 30, 1981
15 yrs. Old

Domino

His coat is black and white,
And he isn't very tall,
He's just a little cow horse,
That sometimes likes to haul.

He's sweet and nice most of the time,
But sometimes he can be mean,
He thinks he's cool and really tough,
But in his mind, it's just a scheme.

He acts like he doesn't like to run,
When all he does is trot,
But if you watch him in the fields,
He's faster than he's not.

He's just an appaloosa,
With a heart as good as gold,
He's just my little appy,
My horse, my Domino.

1979
14 yrs. old

Star In The Night

He's as black as the dark night,
With a star upon his face,
Through the twinkling paths of stars,
His beauty there will race.

He's as fast as the comets that shine,
And streak on through the night,
He goes on forever not stopping,
In an even, steady flight.

His eyes are liquid stardust,
They're as bright as the moon in the sky,
He's like a falling star,
He's clever and he's sly.

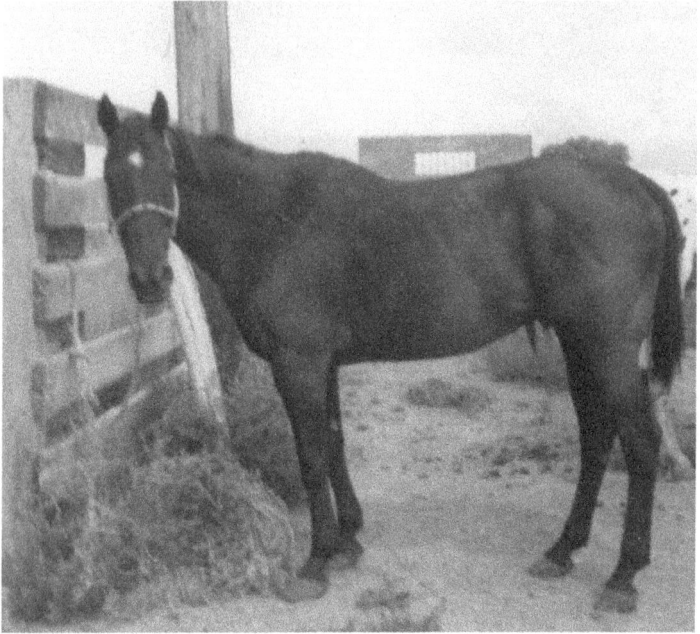

When you look at this beautiful horse,
You'll see an amazing sight,
And the star upon his face,
Is a twinkling star in the night.

1979
14 yrs. old

A Special Dream

I have this special dream,
That is so dear to me,
It is a dream so deep in my mind,
That I hope someday to see.

I hope someday this dream comes true,
I feel it in my soul,
I'll dream it till the day I die,
For it's my last and final goal.

I can fulfill my special dream,
The work is up to me,
But really it isn't work at all,
It's being what I can be.

It's being full of love and kindness,
And not living in vain,
It should all come warm and flowing,
Like a gently autumn rain.

. . .

I won't see my dream for a long, long time,
But I'll see it when I die,
My dream is to make it to Heaven,
Or in hell my soul will lie.

1979
14 yrs. old

Why Do People Fall In Love

Why do people fall in love?
A question that is old,
Is it because that in the heart,
A story is never told?

Or is it because the people around,
Are filled with mixed emotions,
Or is it because there is a spell,
Or the power of a magic potion.

Or is because people need,
Someone to be close to,
Or is it because people just want,
Something they know will be true.

No one knows the answer,
To this one impossible question,
No one knows if in the mind,
It's a thought or just a suggestion.

We only know it's sometimes good,
And everyone falls for it,
It can bring great peace and happiness,
Or it can be the biggest torment.

1979
14 yrs. old

When You Walk By

As I'm walking down the hall,
And I see you coming near,
My heart starts beating faster,
And my eyes don't see to clear.

My eyes are filled with fire,
And my face is one big glow,
A smile spreads from ear to ear,
And I know the fire shows.

As you pass by you smile,
And then you say hello,
And then you walk on again,
And the fire starts to grow.

I feel the blaze grow hot inside me,
And I feel the warmth all around,
Then the blaze dies down to a little spark,
Till you go by again.

1979
14 yrs. old

Remember Me

It's over now,
The time has come for us to part,
You know that I will always love you so.

There once was a time when we were happy,
Walking hand in hand,
When the world was a dream and we were in
    love.

But it's over now, and I love you still,
As I always will,

Please remember me as I remember you.

1979
14 yrs. old

Until Our Love Is Gone

There are so many miles between us,
But still, we are together,
For our minds are filled with memories,
And our hearts and filled with love.

No one will take the place in our hearts,
That we have for each other,
For our love is strong and cannot be
Overtaken by another.

Our love will keep us together,
And our memories will keep it strong,
In our hearts we will be together,
Until at last our love is gone.

1979
14 yrs. old

The Golden Horse

There he stands so tall,
his mane blowing with the breeze,
a stallion of all seasons,
not knowing what he sees.
His muscles are rippling through,
his huge and well-built frame,
I wonder what he thinks of
and does he have a name.
He must have been there forever,
on his face a sad life's stain,
but still, he never moves,
through snow, sun, or rain.

I wish I could go to him,
and tell him he has a friend,
but he's stubborn and will not listen,
the words are lost in the wind.
As I watch in curious wonder,
I know it just isn't fair,
To see the Golden Horse,
on a statue in the city square.

November 2, 1981
15 yrs. old

Rich Man's Death

Satin sheets and silken spread,
Woven lace over a canopy bed.

Walnut chest and redwood table,
Beside the bed, a book of fables.

Red shag carpet and a woven rug,
Bottles of pills and a coffee mug.

Draping curtains, a darkened room,
Shadows on the wall spell certain doom.

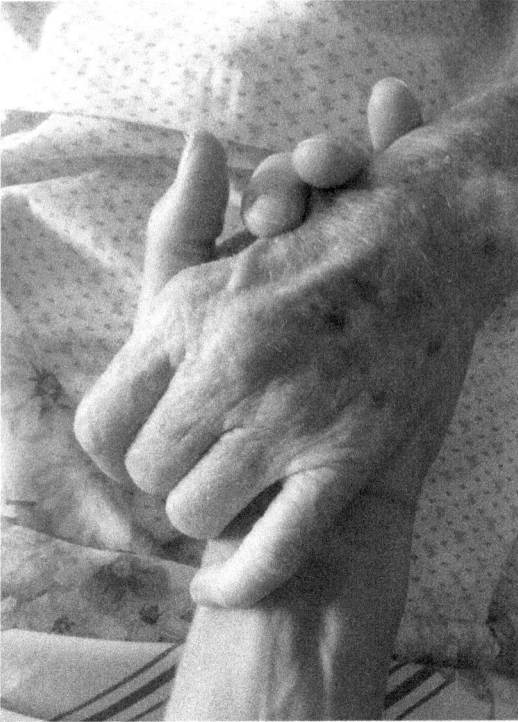

Beautiful paintings hang from the walls,
A burning fire, a charred log falls.

In the bed the rich man lies,
Wishing for love through tear-filled eyes.

Knowing that people only pretend,
Wanting his money, they wait for his end.

March 6, 1981
15 yrs. old

A Dream

I feel as though my life is done,
I'm all closed up, there is no fun,
I wish to cry, to make believe,
My love for you will never retrieve.

A fool was born and that was me,
As blind as I am, I'll never see.
To fall in love is a dreadful thought,
And I feel for you an awful lot.

But you're not the kind who will be all mine,
You won't be tied down, not ever in time.
Why do you make me feel this way,
You laugh in my face, but what can I say.

Please settle down, for I love you so,
But it probably won't happen, a dream, I know.

April 6, 1981
15 yrs. old

The Cowboy And The Bull

No one could ever ride him,
No one could even come near,
The cowboys would always fall,
The run with a trembling fear.
He hooked with a sharpened horn,
He'd kill you if he could,
He was the meanest, strongest bull,
His heart was made of wood.
No cowboy and ever rode him,
Though many of them tried,
They'd usually end up on crutches,
Some of them even died.
He was a big as a two-ton horse,
His muscles were made of steel,
His body would spin and turn,
The cowboys all knew he was real.
Then to the big rodeo,
Came a cowboy from far away,
He had come to ride the bull,
He had heard about one day.

He wasn't very big,
But you could see his body was strong,
He had set it in his mind,
That nothing could go wrong.
He mounted on the bull,
And pulled his rigging tight,
The cowboy's body was tense,
The bull was on the fight.
The chute gate was opened,
The bull twisted and turned,
The 8-second whistle blew,
In the cowboy's ear it burned.
The cowboy jumped off the bull,
He was stomped and kicked around,
The bull was angry and mad,
The cowboy lay still on the ground.
The bull had finally been rode,
Sadness is on his face,
He will never buck again,
The chute is no longer his place.
The cowboy is now dead,
Although his name is famed,
The bull no longer bucks,
His spirit has finally been tamed.

May 31, 1981
15 yrs. old

Daddy

*For the many times we've fought
I love you,*

For all the yelling and screaming
I love you,

For all the sassing and back talk
I love you,

For all the griping and begging
I love you,

For once,

Instead of screaming, sassing, back talking, and
griping,

I wish I would say I love you,

Cause I do.

> *June 9, 1981*
> *15 yrs. old*

My Dad

A cowboy, a rancher,
A farmer, a man,
He's always the best,
Wherever he stands.

He never takes time,
For fun or play,
Except once in a while,
On an occasional day.

He works so hard,
To make better what's his,
And deep inside,
It's for his wife and his kids.

He loves and he hates,
But his feelings don't show,
If you're close to him,
You'll eventually just know.

. . .

He can have a bad temper,
And really get mad,
But I'll always love him,
He's the best; he's my dad.

June 18, 1981
15 yrs. old

My Bay

"Your horse is old and ugly,
you ain't gonna win," they say,
And laughter fills their eyes,
When I show up on my bay.

He looks as though he's empty,
So old he can hardly move,
His bones show through his skin,
You can see every aging groove.

Everyone always laughs,
When I show up at a rodeo,
"There ain't no competition,
she won't win we know."

I just turn my head,
And wait till they call my name,
Then with a burst of speed I'm off,
Their faces grow worried with pain.

I proudly receive my award,
For winning the rodeo that day,
And laughter will fill their eyes,
When I again show up on my bay.

15 yrs. old

Dream

Dream if you think you love me,
Dream if that's the way it must be,
But I don't live in a dream,
I live in reality.

Dream if you think you need me,
Dream and make the night go by,
But I won't be in your dream,
I'll be in your deepest sigh.

Dream if you think you want me,
Dream and you will see,
That I won't be in your dream,
Because your dream won't be of me.

July 26, 1981
15 yrs. old

Little Girl Sweet

Little girl sweet,
Ran away from home,
Oh, Lord, where can she be?
I've looked high and low
For my little girl sweet,
Oh, please bring her home to me.

Little girl sweet
Oh, please keep her safe,
From the things that crawl in the night,
I love her so
My little girl sweet
And my heart is filled with fright.

Little girl sweet
All alone, so afraid,
Not knowing where she be,
Please stand beside her
My little girl sweet,
Hold her hand for me.

. . .

Little girl sweet
She's my whole little world,
Oh, Lord, where can she be?
I sit here and cry
For my little girl sweet,
Oh, please bring her home to me

December 4, 1981
15 yrs. old

I'm Leading You On

Look in my eyes,
What do you see,
It's not what you think,
It's not really me.

Look at my face,
What is it there,
That seems to be moving,
But going nowhere.

Look at my thoughts,
What do they say,
You don't understand,
But I don't care anyway.

Look at my love,
What do I feel,
Nothing unusual,
Nothing that's real.

August 30, 1982
16 yrs. old

The Future

A mound of mud and ash,
Where a cabin used to be,
Everything's dead and gone,
Grass, flowers, and trees.

No animals roam the mountain,
Nothing can be seen,
Only black and barren,
Where it once was pretty and green.

No more cows and calves,
To roam along the range,
Only the scars of time,
That leave an ugly stain.

People no longer go there,
Although a place they loved,
The towers that reach the sky,
They cannot see above.

The giants that cover the mountain,
It seems everywhere they dwell,
But they're not the beautiful trees,
They're the empty oil wells.

February 9, 1982
16 yrs. old

My Star

A look of sadness grows in his eyes,
As if he senses what's going to come,
I think he remembers the old days,
When he was strong, happy, and young.
Even though he's old,
His body is still built to run,
But his legs are crippled and ruined,
And his life will soon be done.
A look of innocence is on his face,
A glow of thought in his eye,
That leads to the depths of his mind,
Where so many secrets lie.
Foundered and crippled, no good anymore,
But his life was not a waste,
He gave all he had to give,
For me, the wind he raced.
Now I know you're dead and gone,
From me you are so far,
But I remember us racing the wind,
And you'll always be my Star.

KELLY OLIVER

. . .

9th grade
About my horse

Grandad

A roughcut man, with common sense,
Who's figured out what life has meant.
Grown old with age, but young in time,
Still working hard and looking fine.
He cares for what's his, and helps it grow,
He's worked hard all his life, and it surely shows.
In old, faded jeans and a flannel shirt,
Up on a horse and covered with dirt.
In a long necktie and tailored suit,
Sophisticated look and shiny boots.
An important man in business life,
He's earned what's his for him and his wife.
A caring man who's made ends meet,
And it'll be a long time till his life is complete.

9th grade

I Love You So

I've never needed anyone
As much as I need you,
If you should go away
I don't know what I'd do.

I love just being with you,
I'm content with holding your hand,
If you loved me like I love you,
My life would be so grand.

But still, it is anyway,
Because I know that you're all mine,
Nothing this sweet can happen,
But once in a lifetime.

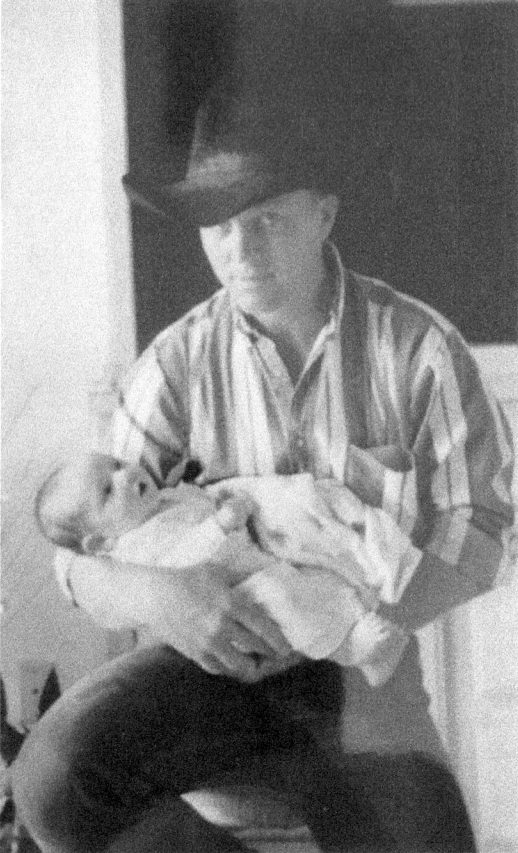

I couldn't live without you,
I hope you never go,
You mean so much to me,
And darling, I love you so.

December 15, 1981
16 yrs. old

The Devil's Steed

His coat is glistening black,
like his flowing, fiery, mane,
He runs free and wild,
for speed and power are his game.

He runs crazy through the wilderness,
like a demon he has fled,
Seventeen hands tall,
and they say he's thoroughbred.

His eyes are filled with flames,
and he breathes fire through his nose,
He kicks and stomps anything in his way,
for in him black blood flows.

There is only one person this horse will obey,
the devil of the dungeon land,
He feeds him fire and hot ash coals,
from the palm of his red-hot hand.

9th grade

Mother

Like the beautiful flowers that bloom in spring,
Like the bubbly waters of a fresh mountain
    stream,
Like fresh alfalfa, and wintergreen hay,
She's always there to say "I Love You" each day.

Like the thunder clouds in a cool summer's storm,
Like the soft falling rain on a gentle Autumn's
    morn,
Like the clear blue sky in the beauty of space,
She's always there to put us in our place.

Like the peace and quiet of a soft winter's snow,
Like the howl of the wind, and the beauty of a doe,
Like a still dark night and a full yellow moon,
If she isn't right there, she'll be there soon.

Her love is always strong,
Like the sun's golden rays,
And mother, although we don't say it,
We think "I Love You" each day.

October 27, 1980
15 yrs. old

You're My Everything

You're my moon on a darkened night,
You're my sun on a cloudy day,
Whenever I get lost,
You're the path that shows me the way.

You're the music in my soul,
You're the melody of my song,
You're the one that sets me right,
Whenever I go wrong.

You're my warmth on a chilly night,
You're my shade on a sultry day,
You're the words that fill my mouth,
When I don't know what to say.

You're the shine that makes me glow,
You're the heat that gives me a spark,
You're my each and every day,
You're the love that fills my heart.

November 10, 1981
15 yrs. old

But Still

Tears will never bring you back,
But still, they always flow,
Memories will never make you mine,
But still, they always grow,
Wanting you will never change a thing,
But still, I always know,
That even though you're gone from me,
I'll always love you so.

10th grade

Grandma

Grandma, a lady, so mighty is she,
I often wonder, if like her, I'll be.
Her heart is so big, I really don't know,
How it holds all the love, that's always a flow
She wants not to take, but always to give,
I think it comes with her desire to live.

She knows all that happens, her mind is so sharp,
And she never gives up on whatever she starts.
She's always the best, and she'll always be there,
And I know in my heart that she'll always care.
Grandma there's something I want you to know:
I'll always love you, wherever I go.

June 18, 1981
15 yrs. old

Rodeo Cowboy

Rodeo cowboy, I love you,
I love your sparkling eyes,
I love the way you smile so bright,
I'd love to call you mine.

Rodeo cowboy, built so fine,
As handsome as can be,
The way you walk, the way you move,
I wish you'd notice me.

Rodeo cowboy, riding bulls,
To see it's a story to tell,
You've gotten thrown, you've gone away,
To Heaven, or to Hell?

Rodeo cowboy, I loved you so
I miss your sparking eyes,
I miss the way you smiled so bright,
I wish I could have called you mine.

April 15, 1981
15 yrs. old

Dear Cupid

You can help me,
Yes you can,
Poke him with an arrow,
And make him my man.

He once was mine,
But not anymore,
But I still love him,
Just as before.

He was my world,
Everything to me,
Let us love again,
Like it used to be.

Cupid, please help me,
I need him so,
All I ask,
Is don't let him go.

February 7, 1982
16 yrs. old

I Remember

I remember how blue the sky used to be,
I remember the grass and beautiful trees,
I remember the flowers, so pretty and tall,
But you went away and took with you them all.

I remember the sun, how it shone so bright,
I remember the moon in the dark of the night,
I remember the stars so luscious and high,
But they went away when you said goodbye.

I remember the birds, how pretty they sang,
I remember the deer in the soft falling rain,
I remember the fawn, so precious and new,
But I won't see them, since I won't see you.

August 1, 1981
15 yrs. old

"I Love You"

Look at my eyes,
Look at my tears,
Look how they say, "I love you."

See how I feel,
See how I need,
See how I say, "I love you."

Watch how I want,
Watch how I cringe,
Watch how I say, "I love you."

Seeing my cry,
Watching me die
Laughing, as I say "I love you."

April 7, 1981
15 yrs. old

No Where To Turn

No one will understand,
So there's no one I can tell,
Things could never get worse,
I'm already living in hell.

No one will see my way,
So there's no one I can show,
There's nowhere left to hide,
And nowhere left to go.

No one would ever help,
So why should I even ask,
No one would even try,
So why take up the task?

Maybe they'd see my way,
And wouldn't be filled with doubt,
I tell myself I'm wrong,
But I'm not waiting to find out.

July 27, 1982
16 yrs. old

Strawberry Shortcake

Strawberry shortcake,
That's all he knows,
Peaches and cream,
Wherever he goes.

Lean sexy body,
Piercing dark eyes,
He can get any girl,
With his soft, pretty lies.

He's a good-looking guy,
Who knows his stuff,
Not one single girl,
Will pass on his bluff.

He knows what to do,
As he plays the game,
Then he'll take her home,
And forget her name.

. . .

One day at a time,
He follows his dreams,
But under it all,
He's not what he seems.

Strawberry shortcake,
That's all he knows,
Peaches and cream,
Wherever he goes.

April 7, 1982
16 yrs. old

Death Run

Through the silent dark forest,
Came a quiet muffled sound,
The sound was getting louder,
And a tremble struck the ground.

Then through the thickened trees,
Came a single frightened horse,
Running to get away,
From a strange and deadly source.

The horse was dark in color,
His body was muscle bound,
He was a great and powerful steed,
No other like him could be found.

His eyes were filled with fright,
His legs were wracked with pain,
But he kept on running hard,
For his life would be his gain.

.   .   .

His sweat was lathery thick,
And he started slowing down,
His legs buckled beneath him,
And he tumbled to the ground.

He heaved and he quivered,
As he gasped his last breath,
But he died knowing he'd won,
He hadn't suffered the devil's death.

9th grade

Maggie

I miss the way you growl and bark,
And like to jump and play,
I miss the way you hog the bed,
And snore in every way.

I miss the way you wag your tail,
When I get home from school,
I miss the way you're always dirty,
And your coat is always dull.

I miss the way you protect me,
When someone is being mean,
I miss the way that I always say,
You're the cutest dog I've seen.

I don't know why you ran away,
But I wish you would come home,
I don't know if you're dead or alive,
Or hungry or all alone.

I only know I love you,
And I think of you all the time,
I hope you remember and still love me,
For I feel the fault is mine.

9th grade

The Beam Of Light

The beam of light
That's oh so near
Is strong and bright
And crystal clear

Floating by
It lingers on
But never sigh
Lest it be gone

It's full of hope
So don't be shy
Just take hold
As it goes by

Don't possess
But don't let go
Not better less
But overflow

KELLY OLIVER

. . .

Hovering near
So strong and bright
Never fear
The beam of light

November 19, 1981
15 yrs. old

Disappointment Valley

There was a place, long ago,
Where I used to run and roam,
A place I'll always remember,
A place I still call home.

Times were always good there,
Even when things were down,
Living in Disappointment,
Was nothing like living in town.

The summers were long and hot,
The winters short and cold,
But I never did grow weary,
Disappointment never grew old.

The valley was hot and barren,
The mountains tall and green,
Disappointment was full of beauty,
Like no place I've ever seen.

Often just thinking about it,
Can bring tears to my eyes,
When I think of old memories,
And long forgotten ties.

I wish I could go back,
To that place long ago,
And relive the happy life,
That again I wish to know.

November 10, 1981
15 yrs. old

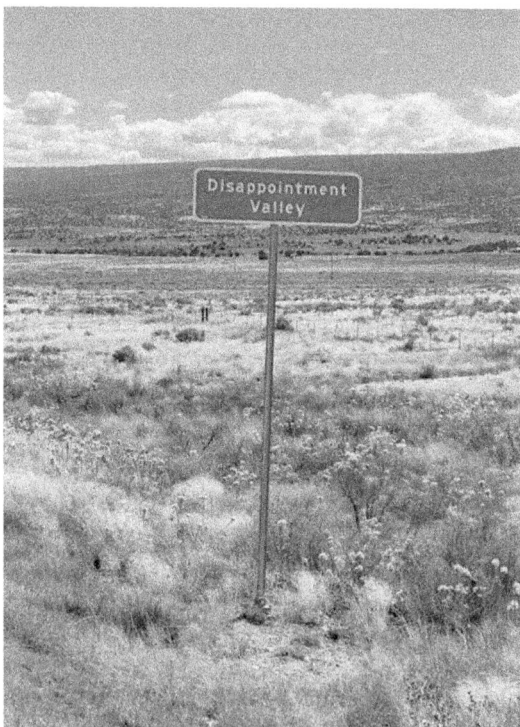

Accept Me As I Am

Do you really love me,
Or am I just a toy,
I wish you'd make up your mind,
Are you a man or just a boy?
One minute you say you love me,
The next, you don't even care,
I'm only alive when you want me,

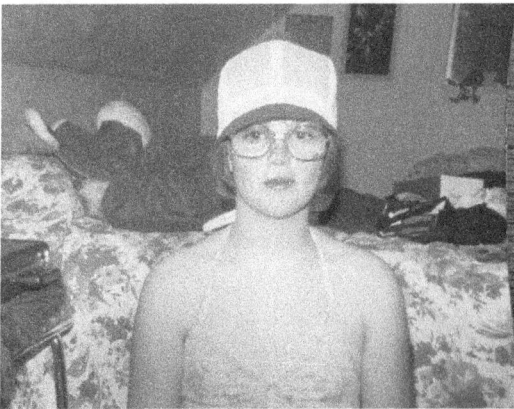

And you know that isn't fair.
You always tell me my faults,
Not matter what I do,
It never seems to be right,
I'm always wrong to you.
You don't like the way I act,
I'm a baby in disguise,
But don't walk all over me,
I'm growing a little more wise.
Something you must understand,
I don't want our relationship to fall,
But accept me as I am,
Or don't accept me at all.

January 24, 1982
16 yrs. old

Win Rhythm

He runs steadily through the trees,
His mane flowing with the breeze,
He runs—with rhythm.

Halting, he takes his ground,
His ears are filled with sound,
He's alert—with rhythm.

In the clearing, another he sees,
There's a shaking in his knees,
He quivers- with rhythm.

He raises into the air,
Pawing at something not there,
He dares—with rhythm.

He charges the other steed,
Gracefully taking heed,
He fights—with rhythm.

. . .

The other comes down on his back,
He feels his strength relax,
He falls—with rhythm.

He takes his last harsh breath,
Knowing he loses with death,
He dies—with rhythm.

The winner stands over the other,
His body is filled, he shudders,
He won—Rhythm.

July 7, 1981
15 yrs. old

Mike Campbell

I didn't even know you,
I never saw your face,
If I did, I didn't know it,
I only knew your name.
I've heard a lot about you,
Of the many bulls you've rode,
You were leading first in state,
From the stories that they've told.
I wish I could have known you,
I wonder who you were,
I've seen the boys on the chutes,
If one was you, I'm not sure.
I didn't see what happened,
And in a way I'm kind of glad,
But if I did, I wouldn't imagine,
All these things that are so bad.
I see your neck torn all apart,
Blood flowing all around,
Your body isn't moving,
You're lying helpless on the ground.

. . .

I want to reach out and help,
But there's nothing I can do,
I just cry and pray to God,
That maybe He'll save you.
It really broke my heart,
When I heard that you had died,
I didn't know what to do,
So I hid my face and cried.
I'll watch the bulls again,
At another rodeo,
And when a cowboy falls,
I'll think of you I know.

May 26, 1981
15 yrs. old

Killed by a bull
Ignacio Rodeo
18 years old

Old Rancher

My bridle's hangin' up,
My saddle's on the rack,
My horse is out to pasture,
"durn this achin' back."

Riden over the ranch,
And workin' in the cold,
I never thought the day would come,
When I'd be getting old.

The great prairie expansions,
Of fenced in golden grounds,
Cattle always a bawlin,'
A rancher's favorite sounds.

Workin' in the blazin' sun,
And cold winter snows,
The hard work of a rancher,
No one really knows.

Finally, the time has come,
When age has brought me down,
"God, you know I regret,
Movin into town."

My bridle's hangin' up,
My saddle's on the rack,
My horse is out to pasture,
There ain't no comin' back.

9th grade

Happy Birthday

I know this will never repay,
The things you gave to me,
But I hope it will explain,
That in my heart, you'll always be.

I know that never again,
Will we ever be the same,
But I think of you all the time,
And I'll never forget your name.

I remember our beautiful love,
And all the fun things we did,
I pray to the stars above,
That someday we'll do it again.

I know I can never forget,
What your love once meant to me,
And every day I regret,
That I ever set you free.

. . .

I long to talk to you,
But there's nothing I can say,
I hope the love comes through,
When I write the words Happy Birthday.

February 26, 1982
16 yrs. old

Sneaking Out

I used to sneak out the window,
Go up town and have some fun,
My parents in bed asleep,
I knew it could be done.

A friend would pick me up,
Or I'd take the motor bike,
But somehow, I'd get up town,
To do whatever I liked.

I'd party with the boys,
And stay out all night long,
Then when morning came around,
I'd sneak in with the dawn.

And then one night it happened,
As I was driving down main,
A car pulled out in front of me,
And I'll never be the same.

. . .

Now I can hardly move,
As I lie here in the gloom,
And I wish there was some way,
To sneak out of this hospital room.

July 20, 1981
15 yrs. old

Larry Don
Motorcycle wreck
July 18, 1981

Larry Don

I saw the lights flashing,
And I wondered who it was,
And then I saw the bike,
That belonged to my favorite cuz.

I didn't want to look,
I didn't know what to do,
So I ran to see who it was,
In case it might be you.

Tears filled my eyes,
When I saw you lying there,
The street was covered with blood,
The sight I couldn't bear.

I wanted to kneel beside you,
And tell you it was alright,
But the words just wouldn't come out,
My heart was filled with fright.

. . .

My mind was filled with thoughts,
Not knowing what to do,
But I finally realized that night,
How much I truly love you.

I gave a sigh of relief,
When I heard you'd be okay.
But I'll never forget that night,
And seeing you that way.

July 19, 1981
15 yrs. old

Rodeo Clown

It was a rainy, drizzly morning,
When National Finals came to town,
I was getting ready to rope,
When I saw the rodeo clown.
He was only a young kid,
Not more than 18 I would say,
And when I looked into his eyes,
I knew something wrong would happen that day.
Although I didn't know him,
I thought I'd seen him before,
I think at once I fell in love,
And nothing mattered anymore.
As I watched the bulls go in the chutes,
I noticed a special one,
A head taller than all the others,
His name they called Shotgun.
I saw a cowboy get on the bull,
Then motion to open the gate,
Then I saw a flash in my mind,
And I knew it was too late.

The bull twisted and turned,
The cowboy was hung up and bound,
Shotgun was ready to kill,
But there came the rodeo clown.
As he struggled to save the cowboy,
He was stabbed with a sharpened horn,
He was flung to the ground,
And the curtain came down,
On the face bloody and torn.
I'll never forget that day,
When National Finals came to town,
And I'll never forget the face,
Of the dying rodeo clown.

9th grade

Best Friends

Times can often be down,
And so often the fault is mine
But you're the best friend that I have,
I need you all the time.

So many times I've let you down,
And treated you so bad,
But no matter what, you always forgave,
Even when you were sad.

You're a friend I'll always cherish,
And never give away,
You're always there when I need you,
Each and every day.

You're someone I can talk with,
To tell my troubles to,
And you're always there to listen,
Whenever I need you.

I hope you feel the same,
And enjoy talking to me,
If I only knew how you felt,
I'd be the best friend I could be.

If ever I lost your friendship,
I don't know what I'd do
Cause there's no one in this world,
Who's as good a friend as you.

9th grade

When A Flower Dies

When a flower dies,
The seed is still alive, hidden underground,
Waiting to bloom again;
Just as my love for you,
Is hidden deep in my heart,
Waiting also, to bloom again.

When all the animals are gone,
Sleeping in the cold of winter,
They are still there, waiting to awaken;
Just as my love for you,
Is waiting to awaken,
When your coolness turns to warm.

When a pond freezes over,
Underneath everything still thrives,
Waiting for the top to thaw;
Just as my love for you,
Still thrives,
Waiting for your heart to thaw also.

. . .

When a seed falls from a tree,
It falls hoping to someday grow again;
Just as I am falling,
Hoping someday your love
Will grow again for me.

March 8, 1982
16 yrs. old

All Out

They came from miles around,
To see the stallion run,
And he'd always win the money,
When the race was finally done.

He was only three years old,
When he started the racing game,
And the people knew who to bet on,
When they heard his favored name.

He never lost a race,
He'd win by at least a length,
His quarter-horse was his beauty,
His thoroughbred was his strength.

He had raced so many times,
To him it was a breeze,
Running had been his life,
And he won with a special ease.

. . .

At his last and final race,
Thirteen horses were in the gate,
He took off like a bolt of fire,
At a unique and powerful rate.

He was ahead by two or three lengths,
On his way to the finishing line,
The fans all knew he had won,
In the fastest and boldest time.

He slowed to a halting stop,
Standing so shiny and tall,
Then the people watched in shock,
As they saw the winner fall.

No one will ever know,
What killed the winning steed,
But they know he went all out,
To fill his master's greed.

1982
16 yrs. old

You're Worth It

It's not worth the shame to sneak,
And see you on the side,
Being near you,
Holding your hand.

It's not worth the guilt I feel to lie,
To see you secretly,
Hearing your voice,
Whispering softly.

It's not worth the trouble I get in to,
Just so I can see you,
Your soft blue eyes,
And silky blonde hair.

It wasn't worth it,
Until you said "I love you."

Things change,

It's worth the shame,
The guilt,
The trouble,

You're worth it,
Because I love you.

April 23, 1982
16 yrs. old

Run Away

We thought we could be together
If we ran away
I remember so long ago
That awful, dreadful day

We were young and innocent
Not knowing all the facts
But we left with happy hearts
Never planning to come back

I remember shining lights
And then a piercing scream
Flames shot up from nowhere
I prayed it was a dream

Kneeling by your side
My heart cried out in fright
Your last words were I love you
Right before you died that night

. . .

Now I sit and cry
Barely making it through the day
We could have been together
If we hadn't ran away

May 4, 1982
16 yrs. old

Sailor Boy

Sailor Boy
He's gone away
To war over the sea
He doesn't know
When he'll be back
A year, two, or three

Sailor Boy
He misses home
He wants to go back soon
He sits alone
Scared to death
That fate might bring his doom

Sailor Boy
He gets the news
In a month he will go home
But he worries still
For until that day
In the battle fields he'll roam

. . .

Sailor Boy
He finally left
He did his duty well
His family got the message
He died
Fighting like hell.

September 27, 1982
16 yrs. old

The Picture

In the picture
On the wall
There is a story
Long and tall

It tells the tale
Of love and hate
War and peace
And life and fate

If you see it
Read it well
It will show you
Heaven and hell

And when you're done
Then you will know
Where you came from
And where you'll go

. . .

So read the picture
On the wall
Read it slowly
And read it all

October 6, 1982
16 yrs. old

Cinderella

Cinderella or cowgirl
Which will it be
Prissy and prim
Or honery and mean

Watching you work
Or working along
Champagne on the terrace
Or a beer on the lawn

Satin and silk
Or an old flannel shirt
Shiny and clean
Or speckled with dirt

Escargot and caviar
Cutlets and veal
Or gravy and steak
And a good homecooked meal

. . .

Cinderella or cowgirl
Which will it be
Prissy and prim
Or just plain ole me

November 2, 1982
16 yrs. old

People

Everybody's different,
But everyone's the same,
People going crazy,
And playing silly games.

Always in a hurry,
And running everywhere,
But when they finally arrive,
They can only stop and stare.

Brainy conversations,
They're all smarties in the head,
But don't take anyone to serious,
They usually don't know what they've said.

They try to find their way,
But they don't know where to start,
It's like a crazy puzzle,
Missing a lot of little parts.

. . .

They climb up to the top,
Only to fall back down,
They don't know where to go,
So they stagger and look around.

They always think they're right,
And they know just what to do,
But if you look inside,
They're as boggled up as you.

November 10, 1982
16 yrs. old

The Sun

Wake the sun, open wide,
Let me see your rays of gold,
In your warmth I will confide,
Till the summer days grow old.

Hold me in your warming arms,
Never let the day go by,
Keep me in your summer charms,
Let me hear your hottest sigh.

Melt the snow and stop the rain,
Bring back the pretty fields of green,
Take away the winter's pain,
Alas, the beauties I have seen.

You keep me happy when you shine,
But sorrow shadows when you hide,
How I wish that you were mine,
Wake the sun, open wide.

November 19, 1982
16 yrs. old

Ricky

There was a little boy named Rick,
One that I loved so,
Everywhere that Ricky went,
I was sure to go.

Ricky came and Ricky went,
But he always did his best,
To show me I was number one,
And never would be less.

Silky hair and starry eyes,
He lit up my whole life,
And I thanked God every day,
That He made him mine.

Only Ricky had the key,
The pathway to my heart,
In the puzzle of my life,
He held the missing part.

. . .

Ricky came and then he went,
He never did return,
Heaven took him back again,
And now the teardrops burn.

My heart's locked up, he has the key,
Never to open again,
He holds a part of my life,
So I can never win.

With Ricky gone I'm nothing now,
Tearstains on everything I see,
I cannot live without him,
So, I'll find him for me.

There was a little boy named Rick,
One that I loved so,
I'm on my way to Heaven now,
I'll follow wherever he goes.

November 30, 1982
17 yrs. old

No Feelings Without You

Where is the warmth?
One day I asked,
For the sun I could not feel,
An illusion in the sky?
But someone said it was real.

Where is the wind?
One day I asked,
As I was standing by the road,
I cannot feel the breeze,
But it was there I was told.

Where is my love?
One day I asked,
As I sat thinking it was the end,
I look everywhere but can't find him,
He's gone like the sun and the wind.

December 2, 1982
17 yrs. old

Take Me Back Again

If I took your love
And cast it to the wind,
You wouldn't try to catch it,
And give it to me again.

If I took your hand
And gave it to a friend,
You wouldn't pull it away,
And give it to me again.

If I walked away
And said it was the end,
You wouldn't ask me to stop,
And take me back again.

But if you took my love
And cast it to the wind,
I would try to catch it,
And give it to you again.

. . .

And if you took my hand
And gave it to a friend,
I would pull it away,
And give it to you again.

And if you walked away
And said it was the end,
I would wait forever,
Until you took me back again.

December 15, 1982
17 yrs. old

Everything Would Stop

If you should ever go away,
The sun won't shine,
And trees wont sway,
Clocks won't tick,
And words won't rhyme,
Glue won't stick,
And bells won't chime.

If you should ever say good-bye,
The wind won't blow,
And birds won't fly,
Dogs won't bark,
And flowers won't grow,
Fires won't spark,
And rivers won't flow.

If you should ever leave me here,
Voices won't sigh,
And hearts won't fear,
Tears would fall,
And souls would cry,
Heaven would call,
And I would die.

January 1, 1983
17 yrs. old

He's Mine

I love Ricky,
Yes, I do,
I love his precious eyes of blue,
I love his blonde and silky hair,
I love his smile that's often there,
I love his subtle sex appeal,
I love the way he makes me feel,
I love his voice, the way he talks,
I love the sexy way he walks,
I love the things he has to say,
I love to see him every day,
I love him because he is so fine,
But most of all, because he's mine.

July 27, 1983
17 yrs. old

Beginning

You never had a past,
And I never had a past,
Our lives began when we met.
Yesterday is forgotten,
And we have the future,
To look forward to,
Together

July 4, 1983
17 yrs. old

Maybe Someday

Maybe someday I'll go away,
Maybe someday I'll die,
Maybe someday I'll travel the world,
Maybe someday I'll fly.

Maybe someday I'll see the moon,
Maybe someday I'll grow,
Maybe someday I'll climb a mountain,
Maybe someday I'll know.

Maybe someday I'll cross the ocean,
Maybe someday I'll be free,
Maybe someday I'll meet the sky,
Maybe someday I'll be me.

Maybe someday I'll know all the answers,
Maybe someday I'll find love,
Maybe someday I'll know where to go,
Maybe I'll find Heaven above.

August 11, 1984
18 yrs. old

Meet Again

Though you will never see my face,
Or touch my hand again,
I'll be with you each passing day,
For my love will never end.

You'll see me in the sunrise,
We'll start the day anew,
I'll be there in the sunset,
To spend the night with you.

You'll hear me whisper softly,
In every gentle breeze,
I'll tell you that I love you,
And put your heart at ease.

You'll feel me all around you,
I'll be in every drop of rain,
I'll lift your weary soul,
And take away the pain.

You'll see me in the clouds,
When you look into the sky,
If you wonder where I am,
I'm the seasons passing by.

Though you won't see my face,
Until this life ends,
I'll be there with you always,
Until we meet again.

September 1984
18 yrs. old

Wedding Vows

PROMISES TO MY HUSBAND

I promise when you're down,
I'll be there to pick you up,
I will hold you,
And comfort you,
And on you, I'll never give up.

I promise when you're tired,
Your needs will always come first,
I will bathe you,
And feed you,
And I'll quench your every thirst.

I promise when you need me,
I'll be there by your side,
I will help you,
And support you,
And bring you strength and pride.

I promise when you're unhappy,
I'll listen while you talk,
I will hear you,
And understand you,
And together many miles we'll walk.

I promise I will love you,
I dedicate to you my life,
Every minute,
And every hour,
I'll be your best friend and your wife.

November 13, 1984
18 yrs. old

My Talk With God

I cry myself to sleep at night,
As I talk to God, my friend,
And I ask the Lord so many times,
When will this nightmare end.

It hurts to see my mother cry,
And at times I feel her pain,
And I wonder what there is in life,
For anyone to gain.

I try to understand it all,
But I just can't see how,
She can slowly fall apart this way,
Letting one man bring her down.

Where once I saw such beauty,
A woman with her head held high,
All I see is loneliness,
And I hear a broken cry.

. . .

I wish there was something I could do,
I tell her that I love her so,
But how can I expect to understand,
Feelings that only she could know.

I wonder what makes love worthwhile,
Is it worth the heartache and pain,
And will it last forever,
Or are all men just the same.

Lord, will I watch my mother die,
Or can she start over again,
Oh God, I pray, just this once,
Please let this nightmare end.

September 5, 1985
19 yrs. old

About My Mother

If I could write a poem about you,
It would tell how beautiful you are,
It would be truer than the blue of the sky,
And have more words than there are stars.

If I could write a poem about you,
The world would know what I know,
That your heart is bigger than the ocean,
And through it your love always flows.

If I could write a poem about you,
It would show that you're special and rare,
The words I would use to describe you,
Would leave no one able to compare.

If I could write a poem about you,
It would say how much you mean to me,
It would show all my love for you,
And that would take a lifetime to see.

November 18, 1986
20 yrs. old

Dear Husband

So often I look into your eyes,
And I see the love that's there,
The tenderness and understanding,
And the warmth that shows you care.

When you take me in your arms,
And hold me close to you,
My heart fills with happiness,
And all my dreams come true.

Your every gentle touch,
Says the words I love to hear,
And your nearness takes away,
My sorrows and my fears.

You fill my every day,
With a love as strong as the wind,
A love that's also solid,
One not even time can bend.

. . .

With you my life's complete,
You make the whole world shine,
And our love can only get better,
As we follow the passage of time.

January 21, 1986
20 yrs. old

My Brother

My brother, but more than that it seems,
For my heart cannot explain,
Battered feelings and shattered dreams.

A closeness, maybe felt by only me,
Brought on by a shared heartache,
That only we can see.

So special, a place in my heart for only you,
It comes from seeing your pain,
When there was nothing you could do.

Alone, by yourself when you needed a friend,
And I only just wanted to be there,
To make the heartache end.

How Unfair, caught in the middle of a
        nightmare,
But I thought of you all the time,
No one could know how much I care.

God, it hurt when I'd see you cry,
And my own tears fell like raindrops,
Till I thought that I would die.

1985
19 yrs. old

The Greatest Gift

In the many years I've known you Dad,
Many gifts you've given to me,
It all seems like only yesterday,
Still fresh in my memory.

You gave me the gift of music,
We listened at night while in bed,
The song "Living in a House Full of Love,"
Will never get lost in my head.

You showed me the gift of compassion,
In Disappointment long ago,
When you told us that our "Apache,"
Would forever in Heaven roam.

You taught me the gift of laughter,
Just simple pleasures at the time,
Like riding in the back of a pickup,
And throwing rocks at signs.

. . .

You gave me the gift of warmth,
You showed me that you cared,
When you gave us the freedom we needed,
To do whatever we dared,

And you gave me the gift of family,
You showed me that love is free,
But the greatest gift of all,
Is knowing you believe in me.

I love you Daddy

May 3, 1992
26 yrs. old

Grandad

There's never been anyone like you,
There's never been a greater man,
Respect is earned,
And you've earned yours,
It's something I'll always understand.

There's a lot of love in this heart of mine,
A lot of pride felt in your name,
But unspoken words,
Are never heard,
I hope you know it just the same.

Someone said to me once, your family is tight,
Oh, but if they only knew,
There's not one of us alive,
Who hasn't asked for advice,
Who hasn't put their trust in you.

You're the smartest man I've ever known,
You've always been there it's plain to see,
When we need your help,
When the blows are felt,
You let us know we've got a family.

I have lots of memories of you,
That I've saved up as I grew,
And unspoken words,
Need to be heard,
So, I want to say, I love you.

August 11, 1994
28 yrs. old

Nana's House

Yoo-Hoo, is anybody home?
Is this the place where there's always a hug,
And a warm and welcome tone?

Yoo-Hoo, this is my Nana's house,
Where we often don't knock on the door,
But sneak in quietly like a mouse.

And holler Yoo-Hoo, is anybody home?

What I remember most about Nana,
Is that she was always there,
And she'd always do anything for us,
To say no, for her, was rare.

And back when we were young,
We'd often spend the night,
And who got to sleep with Nana,
Was the focus of our fights.

She'd sew us our new clothes,
Feed us watermelon on the patio,
Helped us make our garden grow,
And in a little girl's mind,
I knew I loved her the most.

And now I'm all grown up,
The times I see you are fewer and far between,
But I know in my heart if I asked,
You'd still do anything.

And when I come to your back door,
I like to open it up and holler,
Yoo-Hoo, is anybody home?
And I still get my hugs,
And the love you've always shown.

Yoo-Hoo, can you hear my heart speak?
When I say Yoo-Hoo,

I'm saying Yoo-Hoo, I love yooooo.

July 15, 1996
30 yrs. old

My Step Dad

I'm just writing this
Because I wondered if you knew
How dear you are to us
And how much we love you

You came into our lives
When we were already grown
But you made us feel as though
You were someone we've always known

You became my mother's heart
My children's joy to see
Now you're my other dad
On another family tree

You've given all of yourself
You've never let us down
There's nothing you wouldn't do
We love having you around

Thanks for the love you give
Thanks for the patience you show
Thanks for taking us in
And helping as our family's grow

So I'm just writing this
Because I wondered if you knew
How important you are
And how much I love you

February 28, 1996
30 yrs. Old

For Garth

60 Years Together

Mr. and Mrs. Suckla,
Grandma and Grandad, Mom and Dad,
It doesn't matter what you're called,
Hear the respect in how it's said.

Sixty years of hard work,
Love, dedication, and faith,
Has overshadowed all the hard times,
And the heartaches that you've faced.

And though life hasn't always been easy,
You've both always given your all,
At times you may not have wanted to,
But you always answered the call.

You've raised four happy children,
And then grandkids came along,
As you watched your family grow,
You knew life hadn't done you wrong.

And now look how far you've come,
You made it after all these years,
You're surrounded by family and friends,
Who will always hold you dear.

SOME THINGS NEED SAID

So, thank you for your troubles,
Thank you for all you've done,
And remember that we all love you,
And will never forget where we're from.

You make us proud to be Suckla's

2001
36 yrs. old

Like You Nana

Why did it take so long,
For me to finally see,
What I might be someday,
What I want most for me.

I want to be like you,
I want to feel like you,
I want to care like you,
And help everyone like you do,
I want to give like you,
And do the things you do,
I want to love like you.

I took a long, long time,
For me to realize,
The treasure that I had,
Right there before my eyes.

I hope to be as strong as you,
As special as you,
As always as you,
As forever as you,
I hope to be a little like you,
To make a difference like you do,

I hope to be loved like you.

2003
37 yrs. old

Nana's Stroke

Wherever you go, I go,
I'm in your heart and you're in mine,
Over deserts that you'll travel,
Or mountains that you'll climb.

I may not see you every day,
But my love will keep you strong,
It won't flutter when the wind blows,
Or falter when things go wrong.

When God gave me a grandma,
I wonder, what did I do,
To make Him smile upon me,
And bless my life with you.

You've been there for me always,
You mean the world to me,
And when I gaze upon your face,
It's love for me I see.

So, Nana, whatever comes your way,
Everything will turn out fine,
For my love lives in your heart,
And your love lives in mine.

I love you forever.

2003
37 yrs. old

The Angels Sang Today

Even though you've gone away,
The angels sang today.

This pain weighs down my heart,
But the clouds still float up high,
And on the edge of the horizon,
The colors of a rainbow fly.

I can't believe you've left us,
We go on, but still we cry,
And I thought it would rain today,
But the sun still wants to shine.

I thought the wind would howl,
Instead, a gentle breeze,
I tried to hold you with all my might,
But you blew away with ease.

I felt the flutter of a sparrow's wing,
And I heard the Angels sing.

. . .

It must be happy in Heaven tonight,
It's so sad and lonely here,
But the signs of love surround us,
Absorbing all our fear.

And an Angel sang today,
Though we didn't want you to go,
But God opened his arms,
And called you to come home.

And Angels sang today.

September 2003
37 yrs. old

Grandma's Last Words

Our ashes lie beneath the Yellow Rose,
When the wind comes up, we will travel home.

These last few years without you I have cried,
It's been hard here alone, but believe me, I have
     tried.

Lonely tears have filled the corners of my eyes,
But I'm smiling now, for beneath the rose, we lie.

My dreams have been of seeing you again,
My heart was shattered when I lost my best
     friend,

I've looked for you, but you were always a step
     ahead,
Please come back, I can't believe you're dead.

And then, I heard the angels sing,
And sunshine filled the sky,
I took your outstretched hand,
And closed my tired eyes.

Now happiness surrounds me,
Together, we are home,
When the wind comes up, our ashes will blow,
From beneath the yellow rose.

2010
44 yrs. old

A Dog

If I could be a dog,
And my human being was God,
I'd run like crazy with my mouth wide open,
So it always looks like I'm smiling,
I'd stop and smell everything in sight,
And enjoy the world I live in,
I'd lap up the love He gave to me,
And In return I'd be obedient,
I'd have no fear of anything that be,
Because I'd know my God is watching over me,
If I only I could be like a dog.

2011
45 yrs. old

I Made Something

During my time on earth I made something,
I made a family I treasure above all else,
And though I followed in my father's steps,
I made a name for myself.

I carried on my family name,
And made myself an auctioneer,
I bought and sold cattle at the Suckla barn,
And I made myself a career.

Wherever I went I made friends,
I touched lives and people I didn't know,
I worked hard and always loved what I did,
And I made my family a home.

I lived and I loved, and I made mistakes,
Done some things that shouldn't be allowed,
Some of those things brought me shame,
But I still made my family proud.

. . .

Goodbye my friends, Goodbye my love,
Goodbye my precious sons,
Take comfort in knowing I accepted God's grace,
And finally I made my way home.

June 2012
46 yrs. old

About Judd

Last Words For Dad

There were times in my life I struggled,
Trouble and strife had brought me down,
But because of you, Dad, and the love you gave,
I turned my life around.

I came to know my Savior,
I worked hard and the journey was long,
You believed in me and didn't give up,
You were the strength I needed to carry on.

You were proud of the achievements I made,
It was you who helped me get a home,
At times I felt you were my only friend,
You let me know I was never alone.

When you think of me, Dad, don't forget,
That I loved you more than I could ever say,
I've always known that you love me too,
You proved it in so many ways.

. . .

I know you'll miss me, and when you do,
Please don't cry, but wear a smile,
In your heart I live forever with you,
But my time on earth was only meant for a while.

September 2012
46 yrs. old

For Garth
David's words

I'm Not Gone

~

These ashes are what's left of me,
But we both know that I'm not gone,
Take them and make a place to meet,
Where we can talk and carry on.

We'll talk about the good times we had,
And we'll cry and remember the bad ones too,
But you've always been the greatest dad,
I love you more than you ever knew.

So come let's go to that special place,
And say all the things we wish we'd said,
We can never be separated by time or space,
I'm forever in your heart till we meet again.

June 2013
47 yrs. old

For Dad
Judd's words

163

Stella's Eyes,

What color are Stella's eyes? It's something I often
  ponder:
Forever closed in peaceful sleep, now gazing on
  Heaven's wonder.

Do Stella's eyes see Jesus? Do they look at streets of
  gold?
Do they behold the beauty of Heaven that the Bible
  has foretold?

Does she see the perfect rainbow, that surrounds
  God's throne above?
When Jesus holds her in His eyes, does she see His
  endless love?

What does she see in the Light of Heaven, where
  the sun has no need to shine?
Does she gaze upon the Tree of Life, filled with
  fruit of every kind?

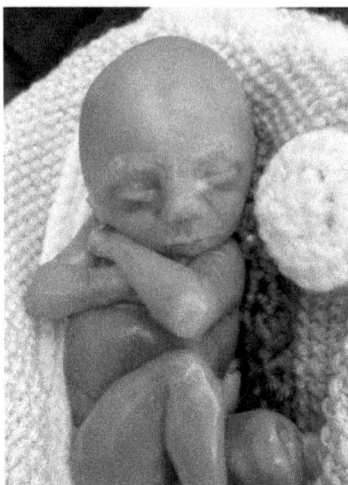

Does she see our loved ones who went before Her?
Do they hold her and rock her to sleep?
As she closes her eyes in Heaven, here on earth we
envy and weep.

All that's left is a broken heart, and a picture
stained with tears,
But her memory lives inside us, and will endure
throughout the years.

I'll love her forever, and never forget her; I'll trea-
sure that precious time:
I'll remember the kisses, the smell of her head, and
the feel of her skin on mine.

Until the day we meet again, and there's no more
reason to cry;
God tells me look up at the starry night sky, and
you'll see Stella's eyes.

.   .   .

Precious Daughter
Stella Marie Harris
March 30, 2023
57 yrs. Old

Kenzie's words

About the Author

Kelly spent her first years of life on a remote ranch in Disappointment Valley in San Miguel County, located about 80 miles from Cortez, Colorado where she was born. Her early years involved the great outdoors, riding horses, being around livestock and playing with her brother and sister and two cousins. Ranch life was isolated but she couldn't have asked for a better way of life. However she always felt lonely and unloved, which she could not explain until as an adult she finally filled that hole in her heart with her savior Jesus Christ.

Always looking for love, even when she had it, always searching for something that couldn't be found, something she didn't even know she needed. Writing down her thoughts and feelings was a way to express herself even if she's the only one who ever read them . From an insecure little girl to a grown woman poetry has always been her way of getting healing and finding comfort in life's ups and downs and hurts and losses.

www.ingramcontent.com/pod-product-compliance
Lightning Source LLC
Chambersburg PA
CBHW060753050426
42449CB00008B/1389